# A BATHROOM
# GUIDE FOR CLOSERS

(RESORT SALES)

*"How to be #1 before you finish #2"*

A guide to getting back on
track in the Timeshare Industry

———

## Todd Speciale
### Christopher Loftis

A Bathroom Guide for Closers
Copyright © 2019

ISBN 978-0-9821002-8-8

# Dedication

I dedicate this guide first and foremost to my wife and children. My wife has stood by me through literally everything. Through the low times, through my many, many, mistakes in life, and without judgment or fear of who we are as a family or where we're going. She's the heart, soul and rock of our entire family. I thank you, my love, for giving me all of you and your support through our growth. Without you, I am LITERALLY nothing.

To my children Averigh, Addyson and Abriella. You girls are the reason Michelle and I breathe. There's not a day that goes by where I'm not BEYOND blessed that God has given me the opportunity to provide for you girls. You make me a better man and life is better with you by my side. Thank you for allowing me the absolute luxury of being your dad. I'm so proud of all of you.

To my mother, MaryJane, who's one of the strongest women I've ever met. You've fought to live, beating cancer more than once. You've fought through trying times while we were growing up to provide a home and food on the table, never complaining about life's difficulties, but instead persevering through them all. Thank you for all you've done.

To my extended family, Art, Karen and Nick Minor for being the additional support always having my back and giving me the strength, I sometimes didn't have to be more than I was. Never doubting me or what I could be, but instead lifting me up and seeing the positives in every move I made.

To my brother and his beautiful family, Rob, Kim, Krista and Tristan, for being a perfect example of choosing faith and family over everything. The lives you lead are beyond impressive, respecting the ups and downs and using each to catapult you to another level of living life on your terms through happiness and love.

To Chris Loftis, a legend in the business who inspired this book, came up with the title, and created multiple collaborative ideas to actually HELP everyone in this business. He's a mentor, a friend and someone who just cuts through all the negativity that this business seems to infect the minds of amazing sales individuals with. He's BAR NONE the best leader I've ever worked with on every level and he KNEW WITHOUT A SHADOW OF A DOUBT that a guide like this was NECESSARY and never done before. Thanks boss for pushing me to do this.

Finally, to my father, Bob Speciale, my angel in heaven who I lost on July 25th, 2017. I promised you I'd keep going regardless of what life threw at me. I promised you I'd touch lives in a positive way and promote REAL CHANGE into those willing to accept it. I promised you I'd always learn, putting ego aside and not allowing any success or failure to change my direction of life, but instead using both to continue stepping forward. Thank you for being the BEST EXAMPLE of love and having our backs without judgement. I love you dad. I miss you, but people will know your name and that it's because when I held your hand the day before you were laid to rest, a fire lit a fire in my soul, like no other, to impact every life I touch as best I can.

For all of you, I'm forever in your debt and will ALWAYS give the best of me to help provide tools that can help others touch the lives of the people they meet, as well as earn a hell of an income along the way!

I love you all,

**Todd Speciale**

Before you get into this guide, (which we know you're going to love) make sure you're ALWAYS motivated and surrounding yourself with positive people. Stay away from industry negativity at all costs. It's a career killer. There are thousands of talented sales agents that are no longer in the business because they let someone steal their dreams and get into their heads. I can remember early in my career when I was bartending, people would always tell me to get out of the business for one reason or another. Looking back, I am so thankful that I ignored the negativity and persevered.

I wouldn't have been able to do this or be where I am today without the help of several positive mentors who believed in me and who taught me to always raise the bar. Thank you Fred Sanstrom, Curt Knipe, Cecil Latta, Mike Tuttle, Rick Lebelot , and Nicki Andreoni. A special thank you to my anchors: my beautiful wife Jeannie, and my daughters, Madison and Grace. They are my heart and soul and what drive me to succeed every day. Last but not least, I would like to thank my mother, Monna Wallace. I owe my work ethic and "anything is possible" attitude to you; always. Love you Mom.

It's about meeting like-minded people and understanding that they just have that drive and gift to want more.  When Todd and I met it was an instant equal respect for one another.  We both have a strong passion for helping others and wanted to do it through raw and real sales processes that aren't necessarily concentrated in corporate environments.  Although their training is essential, this guide is more of what you learn when you hit the floor. These techniques are simple, but needed in a massive way.  We wanted to leave every life we touch, both in the industry and through this book, with the major keys to our success.

Like I said before, keep positive people around you that always push themselves and also push you to grow further every day!  I truly hope…wait let me rephrase that…. I KNOW you're going to get a ton of value out of this guide and wish each and every one of you the utmost success in your careers.

**Christopher Loftis**

# Table of Contents

# Foreword

I've read many "sales books" in my life . . . and have written 24 of them. You might best know me for writing/editing/publishing the best-selling sales training books in "*The Closers*" series.

The difference between this sales training book, "A BATHROOM GUIDE FOR CLOSERS," and most others, is that it caters specifically to timeshare sales; but not exclusively! Because the techniques are as raw and real as they come, they can be implemented in almost any sales process in almost any industry.

Todd Speciale and Christopher Loftis have years of high-level experience in sales. Here, they set out to give you the most important tools possible to not only help you excel at the start, but to get you back on track and keep you there; especially when you find yourself needing it the most. That's something we all experience from time-to-time.

As salespeople, the roller coaster ride of selling can sometimes be shaky - to say the least. But, when you read and apply the lessons in this book, you'll see that it was designed to give you laser-like focus on the most important parts of the sales presentation and process. Not only is "A BATHROOM GUIDE FOR CLOSERS" informative, it reads as if you're sitting in a live training session with Todd and Chris while they are actually teaching.

There's no "fluff" in this book, which is one of the reasons I've taken the time to write this foreword. More importantly, the character of those who wrote this book is one of true professionalism, striving to help others reach their full potential. As Todd likes to say, "Putting the people, before the paycheck!"

I not only recommend "A BATHROOM GUIDE FOR CLOSERS", but I support Todd Speciale, a fellow international best-selling author, life coach and expert sales guru. I also follow him daily on social media and see first-hand how much he genuinely cares! What he's accomplished in his career is remarkable.

And Christopher Loftis is also a leader, expert sales guru, and a person who people believe in and admire on many levels. His illustrious career is nothing short of extraordinary, and was created through hard work and a dedication in lifting others up. You'll see exactly what I mean about both men by the end of this book.

If you have the chance to be a part of their world in any way (as I have), embrace it and come back for more! Enjoy the book and the successes that follow from it!

Read, learn and enjoy!

Ben Gay III

"The Closers" Series

# Introduction

This is a quick guide to getting your mind right and allowing yourself to see the light, when you start to question your ability. We've all been there, including myself. This business is brutal and definitely not for the weak at heart. The only way to stay on track is by going back to the basics, and I don't mean sales tactics. I mean getting to know what made you successful to begin with. We all have ups and downs in life, but we're still here fighting. Why do you think that is? What's your why? How do you find the strength to keep going? Do you have a choice? Yes, you do. You didn't have to read this book. You didn't have to get up today and decide to embrace something that could possibly change your life in a positive way, but guess what.... YOU DID!

I didn't write this quick guide to make a living. I did it because it might just help even one person MAKE THEIR LIVING! "Put the people before the paycheck" has been a motto of mine since day one. What you put out in the world, you get back. Good or bad, it never fails.

So, here's all that I ask, read this guide. Take it in. Use the tools that you already have and at least give yourself a chance to be everything you know deep down inside you can be. There are no new angles, just absolute REAL people, giving REAL value, making REAL change in the lives of the ones you have the luxury of sitting with every single day on the line.

Challenge yourself to think not "outside the box," but "inside the box" of what really works; THAT my friends is being honest and real to each and every family you sit with. Whether you're a Vice President of Sales, Director of Sales, Senior Manager, Manager, T.O., Senior Sales Representative, Sales Representative, Trainer…. or whatever your "TITLE" is…. if you want to see REAL results, REAL paychecks, REAL change, do what the successful honest people are doing in this industry and give yourself a REAL shot at success in a business that can be more lucrative than anything you've ever had the opportunity to do.

I will end this intro with this: I have no college education. I grew up from very humble beginnings. I was a young father. I was in the streets gambling for a living for many years. I thought there was no place for a guy with zero education and professional background, but this business changed my life and it can change yours too. Whether you've been in the business for years or just starting out, at ANY point in your career I hope this quick guide will be a read you use often to get your mind right, and conquer what many can't when they give up too soon.

God bless and here's to the best year you'll ever have in your life, simply because I KNOW YOU CAN DO IT!

Here is a message from **Christopher Loftis**, the co-author and sales guru that's held multiple titles in the timeshare industry. From starting out as a sales representative, all the way up to Vice President of Sales, and has hired and trained thousands in his career. He's also most known for mentoring the right talent and helping promote them to executive levels some thought to be unreachable.

*"When Todd and I first spoke several months ago to discuss this book, we both agreed that unfortunately, most salespeople will not take the time to read a book, so we knew it needed to be concise and to the point. That is how the title and idea of this book was born. In an effort to hold your attention, I won't bore you with the story of my humble beginnings or my lack of degrees. What I will tell you though, is that if I can succeed in this business, anyone can!*

*Here it is, plain and simple…...there is no easy way, or shortcut to success, when it comes to timeshare sales, minimal effort will always reap minimal rewards, as extraordinary effort will always reap extraordinary rewards. But, the key, and the most important tool you can have in your box, every day, is your attitude and your control over it. I have had over two successful decades in this business, where I have encountered hundreds of sales agents with varying personalities and style, and it has been proven to me, over and over again, that having an optimistic attitude is the most important piece of the sales puzzle.*

*It is what separates the winners from the losers, and it is the cornerstone of success in this business. The attitude you project to your clients, sets the tone of the entire sales transaction. Your mood, whether positive or negative, will innately be transferred to the people you interact with. Sales are based on emotions, and positive emotions are contagious. Those who are most successful don't allow for* bad days, or excuses, or problems at home, to manipulate their mindset. There are no bad days for them. It's a discipline that the strongest sales people know how to exercise.

The most successful actively learn the right ways to handle setbacks, they know that they are in control of their own fate, and take responsibility for this control without making excuses. They surround themselves with peers and colleagues that raise the bar, and who live by the same philosophies. It's that simple. Enjoy this book and make sure you take your time reading it. As a matter of fact, we wrote this book so you can read it over and over again for continued growth and maximum value to stay on track at all times! Enjoy!

# CHAPTER ONE

# GET YOUR MIND RIGHT

## CAREER BUILDER OR KILLER: YOUR CHOICE

There's not a day that goes by in this industry where I don't see extremely talented people that don't make it because of their mindset or personal things outside of work. You've got to get prepared! You have to a have a routine to get you ready for the day. It doesn't matter what it is, but it has to be consistent. For instance, I wake up every morning at 5am and write a motivational post and a "Tip of the day" for people in our Timeshare Master Class group on Facebook. I don't get paid for this. I don't do it because I have to, but I do it to keep me focused. My motivational posts are written off the top of my head every morning to inspire me, to keep me sharp and grateful, and to let anyone know who reads it that life's problems can be overcome.

The way I see it, if it gets me started, gets my mind working, and enables me to impact even just one life in a positive way daily, it's a win-win. This is a routine. It's now become habit to write, but I feel extremely good and on point after having to think and get the blood flowing. When I drive to work, I listen to motivational speeches and stories of perseverance instead of music. Those are just my habits and daily routines. What's yours? Do you even have one? If not, get one. This process will change your life. If you listen to motivational stuff, you'll feel empowered and it'll help you through any tough times you're going through.

Which brings me to the "Game Changer" ability. That is being able to leave personal stuff at home and not bring it in to work with you. I know, I know…. it's easier said than done at times, but if you get anything at all out of this guide to success, take this one in. So many individuals bring outside drama to work. You work to get paid and make a good living. You DO NOT go to work to gossip or infect other people with your problems, because the truth is, you're infecting both their mind and your own.

Now how about the complainers. The ones who swear the wheel is being messed with. That they're not getting the best tours, only the top reps are. Well, guess what… even if it is true, those "TOP REPS" we're new reps at one time to also. Shut up, bust your ass and get to be one of those people. Now here's the hard truth, 99.9% of the time, it's not tours being fed to anyone, IT'S YOU!

How about the prejudging, the rotation process, the wave times, the type of ownership they have or if they don't own the market source the tour came from… blah, blah, blah. If you're one of these people, this may not be the business for you. The best reps don't care who they get, what they get, or when they get it. They just write business and assume every family is a sale.

Take accountability! Too many sales people search for new and amazing reasons as to why things aren't going their way. This is complaining and taking zero accountability at its finest. The individuals who consistently PLACE BLAME, rather than ACCEPT it, never last in any sales role with a higher level of efficiency.

Lastly, lose the ego! Someone once said, "Ego acts as a repellent, while confidence draws people in like a magnet." Having confidence is a must. Having an ego will crush your career. Always be willing to help, learn and grow. One hundred percent of the time, when you help someone, you immediately start to grow.  If you're in a slump, you should definitely ask for help, but also try helping someone when you're in a slump; especially if you're seasoned. Lending that helping hand usually reminds you of things you used to do that led you to be successful in the first place. But more importantly, the good will return tenfold just by doing the right thing.

# CHAPTER TWO

# MAKE A CONNECTION

# THE SECRET TO THE SALE

How you introduce yourself matters more than you'll ever know. Are you cold? Are you smiling? Are you prejudging before you meet the family based on their appearance? How's your intent? Does it involve laughter? Do you shake hands with confidence? Do you present yourself professionally? Are you too uptight? Are you thinking about what's going on outside of work? Do you look at a name or where they're from and dismiss the chance of a sale, before even meeting them? ALL OF THIS is a direct factor of why you will or won't close the deal!

How about just forgetting all the tactics or corporate training for once and just try "MAKING A CONNECTION?" Quick question. Do you think you have a better chance at a sale if they like you or if they don't like you? Hmmmm? It's funny how quickly we forget this simple but imperative concept in ANY sales industry. YOU MUST MAKE A CONNECTION!

Make sure they can see, hear and feel how grateful you are that you were the lucky one who got them as your opportunity that day. Make sure they can feel how genuine you are and that you ACTUALLY CARE about them, their family and what's important to their life needs. Make sure that the legacy commitment is met by you, because you genuinely care about how this product will provide a life of memories for years to come to the ones they love most.

This isn't rocket science people; this is just truly being interested in them. And, here's the kicker that most sales individuals forget. It's got to be so REAL, that they feel you

23

care whether…wait for it…. whether they BUY OR NOT! This is the key to every sale. It must be done and it's not hard at all!

You have to remove the sales resistance and barrier that stands between you and who these people really are. How about instead of selling right away, you take time to get to know them. Don't ask them about their vacation commitment out of the gate! Don't have anything scripted so it sounds fake. How about just actually being interested in them? Crazy idea, huh? No, it's the key to every success giant in this industry and it's done through general conversation; letting them speak! Not you; them!

Listen so hard it hurts.  The more you get them to talk, to open up, to tell you about their lives and what's important to them, the more ammo you have to close the deal on the back end. Most importantly, when they feel you CARE, that they're making a friend…wait for it again… whether they BUY OR NOT…. your chances of a sale increase exponentially!

One of the most important keys to success is, to make a friend. Remember, when you want the sale and only the sale, they can see it more than you know, believe that.  Whether you're Front Line or In-House, one of the biggest mistakes people in this industry make is trying to find angles.

Digging a little deeper, we need to establish the importance of making a connection with our clients in order for emotional transfer. The connection you make with your client is more important than the product itself, in your timeshare presentation. People buy from people they generally like and have established a relationship with. But, we have found that not to be enough. As a salesperson, you have to take that one step farther and find something YOU personally like about, and connect to, with your client.

You need to like them, as much as they need to like you, in order for the relationship to not seem manufactured. This is sometimes easier said than done, but it's your job to dig deep and find this information through questioning and discovery. Everyone has something unique about them, whether it be that they are a great mom, have done military service, or that they really like a specific type of music. Find out what this is and talk about it with them. Everyone's favorite subject is themselves, so go with it.

We have definitely written more deals talking to people about their interests, than we have talking about timeshare. This personal interaction will start the process of connection, which will, in turn, lead to the transfer of positive emotions. Don't force it. Be engaged with your client, truly listen, and share something about yourself every now and then that your customer can relate to. Be positive and enthusiastic and make a personal connection they weren't expecting!

This is an EMOTIONAL SALE! Yes, you are selling a great product, that makes sense, but without a connection, you are just *telling* this to you clients, not *selling* it to your clients. Proving your point, and talking about features and benefits, won't get you a deal today. Your job as a selling agent is to transfer positive emotions.

Stop and look at your clients during your pitch. Are their arms crossed? Do they seem defensive and hesitant? Are they looking at their phone and are otherwise disengaged? If so, STOP, you are pitching to deaf ears. You haven't done your job of establishing a connection. We can look around the sales floor on any given day, and with a strong probability, know who is going to buy, and who is not, without being able to hear a word of the presentation. The client's body language and level of engagement tells us everything.

Too many times we see agents that want to get through their pitch by proving a point about the product itself, before making it imperative to establish a connection with their guest. They walk away from the presentation wondering why their client didn't make a fifty-thousand-dollar purchase, with seventeen percent interest, in sixty minutes! Don't be that sales representative! Don't be that T.O. (turn over)! Be the person who undoubtedly understands the MASSIVE IMPACT building that relationship has on every tour.

# CHAPTER THREE

# DON'T FORGET RAPPORT

# BUILDING VALUE IN WHAT MATTERS TO THEM

**RAPPORT:** "A close and harmonious relationship in which the people or groups concerned understand each other's feelings or ideas and communicate well."

Let me ask you a few serious questions. Does it matter if people care or listen to you when you're buying something? Think of a time when you were about to make any purchase, where you felt as if the sale representative didn't care, or that they didn't seem like the wanted to help you. How about even that server who took your order and seem so rushed that you weren't sure if they actually LISTENED to you. How'd that make you feel? When you bought a car, did they take the time to understand your feelings about the purchase? When they were trying to "SELL" you, were you actually listening to them as if they cared or were they just trying to sell you so hard, you weren't engaged because you felt they were all about the close?

Are you building rapport with people the same way you'd like to be sold? Because if not, you're doing what you don't want to happen to you when you're in the market for anything. Have you ever heard of the phrase "practice what you preach?" As sales people, we tend to forget what matters most, and that's actually hearing your guests and what matters most to them; not to you!

It's no secret that we must get clients to trust us and feel comfortable on a timeshare presentation with all the negativity that surrounds this business. If we don't, then guests won't share important details with us, won't trust what we say, and in general won't participate in the sales process in the way that we need them. But how do we build this rapport?

Listening is imperative. Don't just hear what they say. Many sales representatives miss crucial information that can lead to a sale, because they're so consumed with their specific sales process that they forget to actually HEAR what the guests are saying. Before you can even begin your presentation, you need to feel as if you're a part of their world. You know and embrace how they feel and understand what matters to them.

Your speed matters. SLOW DOWN! Yes, we know they're going to try a time close you, but how many times have you had a tour that said, "You've got 39 minutes" and then you're with them for 5 hours? This happens EVERY DAY in this industry. You let them sell you! If you provide enough value, speaking slow and communicating properly, they will make time.

Watch your speed of intimacy also. Depending on the client's culture, background, personality, etc., it may take longer to build the trust required to discuss more personal and sensitive issues. In order to assess the trust level, pay attention to both the content of what the guest is sharing (some guests will only share surface-level details at first) and the guest's body language as they will be important indicators of how much they're ready to share. It is important to be aware of these non-verbal signals because not everyone will clearly verbalize their discomfort.

Remember, your body language, the speed you speak, the way you communicate, the genuine ability to relate and find commonality, is essential to guarantee your ability to build rapport with any guest. Without a strong rapport, your chances of the sale decrease tremendously.

# CHAPTER FOUR

## YOUR STORY MATTERS

## THEY HAVE TO KNOW YOU

Listen, sales is a transfer of energy! If you think for one second that selling timeshare is a logical sale, you're dead wrong. It's 80% emotion, backed up with 20% logic. If the guest doesn't know you, like you, believe you, trust you…. I got news for you. They're not buying from you! I see it time and time again. A sales person goes too quickly into the close, rather than getting to know one another first.

We all have our stories and they all matter equally. If you've overcome something major in your life, tell them. If you accomplished something great, tell them (without being arrogant). If family is your life, tell them. If you love vacation, talk about it and why. If you have a humble upbringing like many, explain why you've changed your life in a positive way.

Your story matters! Once they see you, hear you, and know where you've come from, they'll be open to buy from you. Making stuff up or lying to people about who you were or are, may work on a couple people, but it's pathetic and not the way to achieve greatness. Truth in success is being honest on all levels, especially about who you are and why they should do business with you, rather than the other 40 tours they've taken previously.

Representatives used to come up to me all the time and say, "Boss they just toured 30 days ago and if you look at their history they never buy." My response is, "Yeah, but they've never met you. So, all I need to hear from you is that you're not capable and don't have the sales skills to sell them and then I'll just give it to someone else who can, and you take the hit."

Or, I will hear from an In-House, "Boss, they just toured 30 days ago and if you look at their history they've only upgraded one time." Let me see if anything changes in my response. It doesn't. I still say, "Yeah but they've never met you. So, all I need to hear from you, is that you're not capable and don't have the sales skills to sell them and then I'll just give it to someone else who can, and you take the hit."

Do yourself a favor. Have enough confidence to know that they haven't met you yet. That your story is different, and it matters. You might impact a family's life with who you are, what your story is, where you're from. Do you know how many times I get families that come into resorts and say they're ready to buy, but didn't want to from the previous representative all because they just weren't nice to them? I get it all the time.

Just talk to people. Show them how grateful you are to have them with you and let them get to know you. Don't dive into the presentation without taking some time to get to know one another. Watch how easy they transition to the close on the back end when you do.

Your story matters more to the guest and your process than you'll ever know. Practice it. Tell it truthfully. Be authentic and speak it with conviction. Be proud of who you are and tie it into quality time you now get to spend with the people you value. Just watch how it impacts the sales process.

# CHAPTER FIVE

# KEEP IT SIMPLE

## Less is more.

One of the biggest mistakes sales individuals make in this business is getting too technical, math oriented, or giving so much information that the response you start hearing from your guests is, "It's an information overload." Many of the top writers in the timeshare industry keep it SO SIMPLE that the guests aren't overwhelmed during the presentation. Now don't get me wrong, you need to get "anyway money." You need to follow your process and explain the benefits and features. But, this is an 80% emotional sale and 20% is product. Don't drown them in the technicalities of the program when you can spend more time building the dream and the "why" behind the family time together and memories they're building for years to come by making the decision today!

All too often, sales representatives take too much of the short time period they have with people pitching, rather than getting to know their guests. Usually this ends up with family's time closing you. When you build a solid foundation getting to know them first, rarely do they worry about the time they're with you during the presentation.

When you sit them down and just begin to pitch, it's EXACTLY what they're expecting. You've got to be different! Try ACTUALLY CARING about what matters to them. Try ACTUALLY LISTENING to them, rather than speaking to them. Sales people in this business talk too much. When you keep it simple, you give them time to respond. When they respond, you build your sales ammo on how to close the family. When you listen, they'll literally tell you how to sell them, BUT you have to be genuine and speak with conviction in the process.

The more you listen, the more you bring down the initial sales resistance. The "technical" sales representatives have no idea, but they're actually building the wall of resistance taller and taller when they don't take the time to get to know the people in front of them. Joke with them. Have fun. They're expecting a hard core closer which you can be, but they won't know it.

For example, I worked for a company who was trying to recruit me for over a year. Finally, when I decided to work for them, they gave me an example of what they expected from me. They said, "Where you came from the applied pressure was at a 10 (ten being aggressive closers), there are other companies where the applied pressure is at a 1. We'd like you to help this track grow at a level of pressure around a 5 because that's how we do business. We don't want to be at a 10. We don't want to be at."

I was thinking about that statement and replied, "You didn't try to hire me for a year to keep consistency at a 5. We need to train this track and it's 145 representatives, 20 T.O.'s, 4 managers, and 2 senior managers to STAY at 5. You need to sell at an applied pressure of a 10 and make it FEEL like it's a 5. That's how you thrive in sales!" The Vice President thought about it and told me to do what I think is best. We doubled the sales efficiency in less than 7 months and everyone grew to levels this company had never seen before.

What's the moral of the story? Push but do it where it feels light and easy. Give the guests an experience they're not expecting. Build the dream. Find the why. Allow them to ease into the sales process. Don't force them in like they're used to.

LESS IS MORE! You're going to give it all you've got, but just do it while having fun and using $3^{rd}$ party stories on how this product, the experience it gives families, and how it will impact their family's lives when they decide to get involved. Try it. You'll see an immediate impact in your closing, VPG (volume per guest), and your average sale price in an extremely positive way.

# CHAPTER SIX

# ANYWAY MONEY

# How REAL is it?

"Anyway Money" is money guests are guaranteed to spend on vacation whether they purchase your product or not. How important is the "anyway money" to you? It's one of the most important pieces of your presentation. It's often the key to closing the deal, but only if it's REAL. Let me say that again......ONLY IF IT'S REAL!

The problem with most sales individuals in the timeshare industry is they rush through the "anyway money." Worst decision ever. Guests have to OWN their "anyway money." They MUST tell you that they spend the money or are going to spend the money (i.e. retirement/planning for the future). Also, I recommend that you use a range of what they spend instead of listing out how much they spend per category. When you list items out, it gives people too many ways to say the word "no" to certain things.

Here's a couple of examples of what most representatives do:

### Example 1:
Rep: "How much money per year do you spend on…?"
1. Hotels
2. Car Rental
3. Airfare
4. Cruises
5. Food
6. Entertainment

Guest common response: "Well we don't hardly ever stay in hotels. We drive our own car. We fly the cheapest airlines, so only couple hundred per year. We hate cruising.  We cook our own food, but if we do go out its at cheap places so $100. And, we just hang out by the pool."

### Example 2:
Rep: "How much are you spending on vacations per year?"

When you do this, you give the guest too many ways out. They can reply with many answers that don't help you get down to the real money.

Guest: "We really don't vacation much," or "We don't spend money while we vacation. We just hang out as family."

### Example 3 (The right way):
Rep: "If I were to ask you guys how much you're currently spending on vacation per year now, most families are spending between $5,000-$10,000 per year, inclusive of all hotel stays, car rentals, airfare, cruises, food, entertainment and more. Where would you fall? Are you closer to $5,000 or $10,000? *(Wait for the guest reply. DON'T SPEAK.)*

Guest: "Well that's hard to say."

Rep: "Well just a conservative number that you know, God willing you're healthy, you have a job and money's coming in... what's that number?"

Guest: "I've never really added it all up." *(huge chance to plant a seed of why vacation ownership is so important.)*

Rep: "I completely understand and that's a common thing for people to say, because you spend $200 here, and then $100 there, and then $800 for airfare, and then another $200 on car rental. Like you, most people don't really add up their ENTIRE vacation costs because they're only spending it a little at a time or once a year. There's two things people say when they really dig deep and find out how much money they're **REALLY** spending per year on vacation. They either say, "Wow, I need to stop vacationing," which never happens, or they say, "I need to figure out a way to REDIRECT *(awesome word)* these vacation funds into something that will save me money, keeping costs down and give me more value in the future." So what do you think a **REAL**istic number is that you're spending per year on vacation? Like I said, for most families, including all of their travel costs, that numbers usually between five and ten thousand."

**SIDE NOTE: Yes, I just repeated myself again. You're planting seeds that allow you to get people to say what you'd like them to say. For instance, when I use $5,000 to $10,000 and say, "Which are you closer to?" It's guiding them to either, and both are good numbers for a vacation commitment. If they say the low end, that's still $5,000. You'd then reconfirm $5,000 is what they mean. Now, had I said $2,000 - $5,000, they could've easily said the low end again and now I'm getting 1/3$^{rd}$ of the vacation commitment I have at $5,000 just for**

**"suggesting numbers" which is a HUGE tool in this industry.**

Guest: "I'd say the $5,000 range."

Here's where most reps make the biggest mistake. They just *accept* that $5,000 number. That's not a real number until you've confirmed it multiple times and made them say it. After they say it, you write it down, circle it, write "REAL" next to it and circle that. You get the picture? And, NO I'm not kidding or exaggerating. Do it that much!

Rep (wrong way): "Ok, sounds good." *(and they move on)*

Rep (right way): "Ok great. So, you're spending $5,000 a year on your vacation costs. Now that's 100% **REAL**. God willing you're healthy and money's coming in, right? Because here's why I like to GUARANTEE this money is real. EVERYONE hates to be sold, everyone, including me. You don't know me, and I don't know you. You could lie to me and say you spend $1 a year on vacation or you could tell me the truth. I could lie to you and tell you our product is perfect, but it's not. The ONLY THING that doesn't lie is a calculator. So, here's what I'm going to ask you to do for me. DON'T – LIE – TO – YOURSELVES just because you don't want to be sold. *(Insert third party story about when you promised you weren't going to buy something, but you did because it made too much sense to do it financially and it added value to your life.)* **BE REAL** on how much money you're spending, because you have to be here

50

anyway. If I could possibly save you and your family thousands of dollars for years to come, whether you buy or not, it would be at least worth listening to what I have to say. Wouldn't you agree? So once again, the $5,000 you just told me, that's 100% A REAL NUMBER that you're spending every single year on a conservative level, right?

Guest: "Yeah, that sounds about right." *(STOP! "About" is not ok.)*

**SIDE NOTE: READ BODY LANGUAGE AND FACIAL EXPRESSIONS. They look at each other. The wife's face says yes, the husband's face looks like it's still a little high or they make a sound like "Mmmmm, not sure," STOP and reconfirm until you get a solid number.**

Rep: "Ok, Mr. and Mrs. Jones, it sounds like you're still hesitant on that $5,000 number and I want a number where you're 100% sure. So, if I said something like *(suggestive numbers)* $4,500, is that a number where you BOTH are going to agree you'll be spending per year on vacation? Like at least $4,500. Could be more, but at least that?"

Guest: "Yes, that sounds *more like* what we'd both say is a number we'd spend every year no matter what."

Rep: "Are you sure, because I can't have you tell me you may, or MAY NOT spend this money at the end of the presentation, so are you 100% sure that's a 'conservative' number you're going to spend annually?"

*SIDE NOTE: YES, I keep repeating myself. Sales is psychological. Repeat yourself. They'll listen and understand more, and you can guide them to any destination when you do, but MOST IMPORTANTLY during the ANY WAY MONEY, they'll say it so often they'll truly hear themselves and believe that's their number. When they SPEAK IT, THEY OWN IT! They can't sliver their way out on the back end, like a lot of representatives allow them to do.*

Guest: "Yes, we BOTH are sure."

Rep: "Sounds great. So, $4,500 no matter what every year. Ok, I got it. Now let's see how we can help you. This product may or may not be for you, but at least now we have a GUARANTEED 100% **REAL** commitment to spending time with the people you love most and that already is an AMAZING choice. I really want to commend you guys for doing that."

Here's the deal. You need to COMMEND and COMPLIMENT them on spending the money they do with the people they love most on vacation every year. You're literally confirming why it's important to do so, but they'll also tell YOU when you compliment them how important it is to them as well. This is also RE-CONFIRMING why vacationing is so important to them.

Now, what if they truly just started vacationing and don't really have any "anyway money?" Most representatives just spin the tour and don't give it a show. One of my biggest deals ever was from building the vacation commitment on what they'd LIKE TO DO when they retire, and we spent 30 minutes on that cost 15 years from now for 6-8 weeks a year. I used what they know to be a cost for a week of vacation for them now and then I asked them…wait let me say that again…. I ASKED THEM *(I didn't tell them)* what they thought that same week would cost them 15 years from now. I multiplied that, by the number of weeks they wanted to travel when they retire and made them repeat that number to me over and over.

I spoke about why it's important to save, not to plan, for the future. For instance, if we're smart we ALL are planning for the future. We are taking GOOD MONEY out of our pockets right now, and are putting it in stocks, 401k, IRA's, mutual funds and more for the what? It is FOR THE FUTURE. A lot of those investments we can't even touch until we're 59 and a ½ without a tax benefit, but yet we still do it. Why is that? Because we know prices are going to go up. We don't want to work forever and we need to save money to do the things we want in the future. You don't HAVE TO invest or save money. You could've spent it on another suit, a watch, a car, whatever you wanted to. But, you didn't. You saw the value in taking money out of your pocket today for FOR THE FUTURE!

HELLO! If your guest doesn't relate to the same concept, you missed something. This is the same thing. You're taking good money out of your pocket, guaranteeing you to save money and do the things you love to do in the FUTURE, because you're smart enough to plan now; so you can reap the fruits of your labor while the money's coming in.

I really hope you see how important this section of your presentation is. I wanted to spend a little time on the "anyway money," because if it's not a **REAL** number, then the number you get from them is really worthless. You shoot yourself in the foot when you don't get a TRUE commitment on this.

You give them so many ways out on the backend when you just accept a mediocre vacation non-real commitment, such as:

1. "Oh, well we don't spend that much every year."
2. "Well yeah, but that number is ONLY IF we go on vacation and we don't every year."
3. "Oh, that number was for the whole family. We don't travel with them all every year." Etc...

You guys get my drift, right? When they SPEAK IT, THEY OWN IT! They can't say any of this when they're re-confirming their own number.

Be smart on this section of your presentation. This is not a part to take lightly. Selling is a transfer of energy on all levels, but you must have them committed to vacationing and to the cost. It ALWAYS comes down to the money!

# CHAPTER SEVEN

# BUILD VALUE

# INSTANTLY & THE FUTURE

This is a part of the presentation where people drop the ball way too much! You must build value into your product in the guests' eyes, or the chances of selling them are going to be extremely slim.

For instance, if I asked you to choose any exotic car in the world that you could own what would it be? Ok, you got it? Now what if I told you that you could own your dream car for $25 a month, would you buy it? I know you said, "YES." You want to know why? Because, NO ONE EVER SAYS NO for $25 a month. IT'S AFFORDABLE and we haven't even talked price or terms yet. On a serious note now, why is that? It's simple. I asked you about something you ALREADY SAW MASSIVE VALUE in owning, but there's only one thing that stops you from really ever obtaining what you want and that's MONEY/COST.

In this example, you would not care if your exact dream car was 25000% interest and the sticker price to purchase it was $9 billion. For $25 a month you'd still buy it, and that car would literally rot in your driveway, your kids drive way, your grandkids driveway, and your great, great grandkids driveway. You know that's true too, because the MONTHLY cost made too much sense, and you see so much value in that car that you would simply never say no!

Your product is the same way. If you spend enough time building value in what this product can do for them, how it can change their life, and their family's lives for years to come, leaving a legacy of happiness by making a decision *(when?)* TODAY, then you're always going to give yourself the best chance at a deal.

Tie third parties' stories into your value pitch. I always said, "Look, I KNOW I'm not going to be able to leave thousands of dollars for my kids when I'm long gone, but if my daughter is a gas station attendant and that's what TRULY makes her happy, then I'm happy for her. The truth is, will being a gas station attendant give her the means to travel all over the world and see the things that she may want to see? No. It most definitely won't, but knowing that I'm leaving this for her and that every time she travels she'll be thinking of me, that's what makes me know I made a life changing decision, bringing pure happiness in their lives, by giving this to my kids."

You have to find the dominant buying motive (DBM) in every sales presentation and that's through VALUE of some sort. Value is defined differently for each family you meet. Finding this out through discovery and planting seeds that directly connect to something that has value to THEM is very important. Some see value as dollars. Others see it as quality time with the ones they love most. My kids, literally, don't remember what I got them for their birthdays or Christmas 4 years ago. But, they remember exactly where they were on vacation, and the memories that come with it.

It's imperative that while building monetary value that you don't EVER elude to a drop. People in this industry build value and then try to close improperly on the "what if's." What I mean by that, is that you spend a ton of time building up the monetary value of what you're selling and then say something like, "If it were less, it'd be a no brainer." There's a time and place to use this mini tie down, but it's NOT when you're building the monetary value of your product. This is more towards the back end when speaking on the difference between the "anyway money" and ownership.

Without the guest seeing the value through the product, the legacy or IN YOU, you're simply limiting your opportunity to close the deal. Take your time and make sure the connection is REAL on how important it is for them to understand how owning can impact their entire family in an extremely good way. With this, you win. Without this, it's much more difficult to be at the top of your game or this industry.

# CHAPTER EIGHT

## TAKE IT AWAY

## THIS ISN'T FOR EVERYONE

What does it really mean to "take it away?" This is a tool used by advanced sales individuals in this business. The truth is, most are too afraid to even use this tool that is absolutely essential to your success. Many guests will come to these presentations and already have a "game plan." They are ready to be sold at every point in your presentation. Box and close, box and close. This is what they're used to. This is also a huge reason why one-dimensional sales people don't even give themselves a chance to grow or close more deals.

Why? The importance of the takeaway. It boils down to the saying, "Everyone wants to buy something, but no one wants to be sold." Think about what is going through the guest's minds.

When you're in your element pitching and you feel like you're getting resistance at any level, the takeaway is a tool most families don't expect. Fear of loss is more powerful than you can ever imagine. There are SO many people that won't allow their ego to get crushed. I've personally sat with many guests that say over and over and over again how they aren't purchasing anything today *(which by the way are the best tours)*, but after you do a simple little take away, such as:

*"I completely understand that sir. This product isn't for everyone. It's very expensive. Some can't afford it. Some can't…. Either way we are blessed to have you here today."*

*"I'm assuming that based on the fact this is what is already coming out of your pocket, then this is a number that isn't taking away from any other goals you have in life: like paying for education, saving for retirement, renovating the house, or anything else, right? Because if it is, I'd tell you not to even consider ownership. Now, unfortunately we don't have anything in that ballpark, but just to see if we're on the same page, if we did have*

*something that was in that range and it gave you more value it would be an absolute no brainer, right?"*

*"Sir/Ma'am, you're obviously super smart when it comes to numbers. At this point it should be extremely clear that the value is there, and unfortunately if it's not, I've failed you and I'd be more comfortable if I just closed you out."*

Just that verbiage alone, will crush an egomaniac. The words "some can't afford it" is a blow they don't like to endure, but you MUST follow it up with a very simple "either way we are blessed to have you here today," which is all very true. You poke and then compliment. Poke, then compliment. Repeat this process as needed.

Understanding timing on when to do a takeaway is solely at your discretion, but usually found out by reading how the guest is taking in what you're pitching. Read their body language, facial expressions, and LISTEN CLOSELY to every response they give you during the key points of your presentation.

The natural human instinct is to say "No" to anything new and seemingly unneeded. It goes far beyond sales, but more into the human psyche. The human instinct is to stick with the status quo. It's a form of self-protection. So, what we have to do is be the opposite of what they're expecting. We have to find the balance of selling them but also in a weird way, give them "the out" and address the fact that it's okay to say "No," and even give them the reasons why they should. This will completely throw them off their game plan and send confused signals to the brain that isn't sales resistance, but that of confusion and now trying to read a new situation. Sales resistance naturally decreases when they aren't so focused on their game plan of saying "No" and now more focused on trying to read the new situation and listening to what you have to say.

This strategy, ironically, takes power away from them, and also gives them power at the same time. The power you're taking away is their resistance. You are now in control; they just don't know it. But, in their mind, they have gained power with you giving them the ok to say "No." This is one of the most powerful tools in sales psychology.

In the end, you just CAN NOT BE SCARED to take it away! Try it on your next table. Stop selling and use this powerful tool and see how impactful it is. You'll be thankful you did.

# CHAPTER NINE

## USE YOUR AMMO

## HERE'S WHERE WE CLOSE

At this point, you should have all the ammo you need to start firing. Knowledge is key and understanding how to use that knowledge is equally as important. It's way too easy to just say, "You're spending this _____, so you should buy this." I wish the sale process were that simple, but it is not.

Everyone has a DBM (dominant buying motive) and an EBM (emotional buying motive). Using these two is key to guaranteeing yourself the best chance at closing the deal!  Get back to the key factors of WHY they vacation. What were the reasons that stood out in the sales process that perked their interests the most? Was it being able to go on that dream vacation? Was it being able to give their kids life experiences and opportunities to travel that they themselves never received as a child? Was it how much money they'd save for future vacation costs? Was it the ease of how simple it would be to book their vacations anywhere in the world?

There may be many other reasons they are interested in your product, but being able to signify the ones that meant the most to them, is what's going to get you the deal every single time. You have to put your ego aside at this stage of the presentation. Read this next sentence carefully:  IT'S ALL ABOUT THEM!  This is a sensitive time where you have one shot to GET – IT – RIGHT!

Too many sales individuals in this business start re-covering what they've been going over for the last 60-90-120 minutes. WRONG! This is a time to present an option and shut up. Don't talk too much. If you present a price and just listen, they'll tell you how to sell them. They're going to throw blanket objections (anything they can think of to say no) that really have no substance to the real reason they're not trying to buy. If you listen, you can find the REAL objection. After you've dropped the first numbers you're going to get things like:

Guest: "There's no chance I'd pay that interest rate."

Sales Rep/T.O.: "I understand Mr. Jones. If the interest rate was something that suited you, can I welcome you to the family?"

Guest: "This product is way too expensive."

Sales Rep/T.O.: "I understand completely Mr. Jones. The product is a large investment, but if it were the SAME MONEY, which obviously, it's not, but IF it were the SAME EXACT MONEY you're spending now, and you could just redirect that money to our ownership, you'd obviously become part of the family today, right?"

This is called a "temperature check." You can have all the ammo in the world, but remember, the only ammo that matters is the ammo that matters to them most. They're going to try and wiggle out on the back end. What you're doing in the examples above, is finding out if the objections they're giving you are the REAL ones. A little "I understand" acknowledging that you hear what they're saying and respect it, followed by a mini "if I could, would you" trial close, will immediately tell you what the real objection is. Little hint: DON'T WASTE TIME ON THE WRONG OBJECTION!

Way too many sales individuals and T.O.'s in this business waste valuable time on the back end. The guest throws a "No I wouldn't because…" out there and they try and handle an objection that would never get them the sale anyways. Your ammo (key power reasons why they'd buy) has to be recognized and used on the back end to trial close through the information they gave you throughout your sales process.

One last piece of advice: Don't get frustrated with them at this point when they say no. It's expected. You know it's coming. If this job were easy, everyone would be rich. Do you have any idea how many times I've heard this: *"The sales rep or manager was really, really nice, UNTIL we said NO. Then it was like a whole new person was sitting with us. They were mean and defensive and basically telling us we were stupid not to buy."*

If I can teach you anything, getting rattled will guarantee only one thing in this business: absolute failure to succeed at an optimal level. Keep your mind right, your temper in check and always, always, always be kind and courteous to your guest. You want to sell more…. JUST BE NICE!

# IN CLOSING

# KEY TIPS TO YOUR SUCCESS

Don't be that person. You know the one I'm talking about. The person who never helps anyone else. The person who never wants to share information that will make others successful. The person who hates when others do well, but fake that they're happy to their face. Don't be the person that thinks they know everything. Don't be the person who hates to train. Don't be the person who is arrogant or thinks they're above others. Don't be the person that talks shit about others.

People that don't want to help others are weak and obviously don't have a clue at how it comes back around in many ways. Share ALL the information you have that will help others succeed, because when you need it, they'll be the first to come your way giving back what you gave to them.

People that hate on the success of others, are truly just masking the real problem within. It's having the lack of confidence to do what others are doing. BE REAL ALWAYS! Be genuinely happy when people succeed on any level. The inner gift of wanting everyone to do well, will also come back tenfold; I PROMISE!

People that think they know everything ABSOLUTELY DO NOT! This is usually an ego problem. They've been in the business too long. They hold a title above you and feel because of that they can't learn anything from you. Listen clearly now to what I'm about to say. YOU CAN LEARN SOMETHING FROM SOMEONE THAT'S BEEN IN THE BUSINESS ONE DAY OR 50 YEARS! You never ever stop growing. Keep your mind open to always learn more. The sales process changes in time, and so does the clientele.

People that hate to train, never really give themselves a real chance to excel and grow to levels they once thought unreachable. THIS IS HOW YOU GET TO THE TOP! Train! Train! Train! Train inside your company, but it's IMPERATIVE that you find fresh outside training courses to give you new perspective on how to stay at the top of your game. There are many choices. Invest in yourself, it's the reason why the best are the best!

People that are arrogant or think they're above others are like a cancer in any sales environment. They poison the atmosphere and it affects mindset and the ability to create a culture where positivity rises. LOSE THE EGO BRO! Life is too short. No one person is better than another. That's how you sell, work, live and lead!

Keep your thoughts to yourself. You don't want to be the gossiper. This is the quickest way to lose respect, and more importantly opportunities to grow within your company and further. Help people, don't exploit their faults or failures. Always strive to be a better version of yourself. If you have an opinion, like we all do, keep it to yourself. I've seen it backfire all too often. Oh, and one more thing, if you think you look cool because you have the latest information on someone who's made a mistake or failed in any area, YOU AREN'T cool and you look like a complete asshole to the masses. Just sayin'.

Finally, I'll leave you with this: This business is EXTREMELY TOUGH! I've seen people make millions and I've seen people get crushed. The difference is mindset and the willingness to do what it takes to succeed and do it RIGHT! You don't need to lie to sell. Don't worry about where you're at on rotation. Don't worry about what type of tour you have. Don't worry about who's being fed. Don't worry about that one person who the boss favors over you. Don't sweat any of this bullshit! All you're doing is clouding your mind. You're sacrificing your sales ability, and the only person questioning the process is you! Don't listen to others that constantly complain (i.e. the rep room).

Keep your mind right and your head strong and you'll do just fine. Be the motivated, positive person who looks for the good, be thankful for every tour you get, and follow the right routine that gives you the best chance at success. Gratitude is more powerful than searching for the bad EVERY SINGLE TIME!

I wish you the utmost success and I hope you enjoyed these tips to success. If you have enjoyed this, share the book with your co-workers or anyone looking to grow. Remember, assisting others is a feeling like no other, and is more powerful and valuable than any paycheck you'll ever receive. I dare you to try!